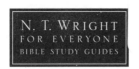

N. T. WRIGHT
FOR EVERYONE
BIBLE STUDY GUIDES

1 & 2 THESSALONIANS

8 STUDIES FOR INDIVIDUALS AND GROUPS

N. T. WRIGHT

WITH PATTY PELL

IVP Connect

An imprint of InterVarsity Press
Downers Grove, Illinois

InterVarsity Press
P.O. Box 1400, Downers Grove, IL 60515-1426
World Wide Web: www.ivpress.com
E-mail: email@ivpress.com

This study guide is based on and includes excerpts adapted from Paul for Everyone: Galatians and Thessalonians, *©2002 Nicholas Thomas Wright. All Scripture quotations, unless otherwise indicated, are taken from the New Testament for Everyone. Copyright ©2004-2008 by Nicholas Thomas Wright. Used by permission of SPCK, London. All rights reserved.*

InterVarsity Press® *is the book-publishing division of InterVarsity Christian Fellowship/USA*®, *a movement of students and faculty active on campus at hundreds of universities, colleges and schools of nursing in the United States of America, and a member movement of the International Fellowship of Evangelical Students. For information about local and regional activities, write Public Relations Dept., InterVarsity Christian Fellowship/USA, 6400 Schroeder Rd., P.O. Box 7895, Madison, WI 53707-7895, or visit the IVCF website at <www.intervarsity.org>.*

Cover design: Cindy Kiple
Cover image: Photos.com

ISBN 978-0-8308-2193-8

Printed in the United States of America ∞

| P | 18 | 17 | 16 | 15 | 14 | 13 | 12 | 11 | 10 | 9 | 8 | 7 | 6 | 5 | 4 | 3 | 2 | 1 |
| Y | 24 | 23 | 22 | 21 | 20 | 19 | 18 | 17 | 16 | 15 | 14 | 13 | 12 | 11 | 10 | 09 | | | |

CONTENTS

Getting the Most Out of Thessalonians

I hesitated long over the decision. I had to make up my mind whether to admit to the university a student whose grades were not quite as high as we would normally require. She was clearly intelligent, and capable of hard work, but why were some of the grades just a little bit lower than we had expected?

Then I thought back to the interview my colleagues and I had had with the student. She had come alive. She was clearly not only interested in the subject, but enthusiastic, and able to take in new ideas and make them her own. Remembering those first impressions vividly, I made the decision. We would admit her to the college. Three years later I was vindicated: she graduated with top honors.

Paul vividly remembers his first impressions of the Thessalonian Christians to whom he writes. (The story of his encounter can be read in Acts 16 and 17.) They would suddenly understand what he was saying. It would grasp their hearts and minds. Paul and his companions, explaining the gospel to them, would become excited as they saw the message take hold, make sense, and begin its work of transforming hearts and lives. That memory lingered on even though Paul, Silvanus and Timothy had moved south, to Beroea, Athens and now Corinth. (Paul doesn't say so in the letter, but it is likely that he was writing this from Corinth, where he stayed for over two years.)

Paul's two letters to the Thessalonians are among the first, perhaps

the very first, that Paul wrote to the young churches of the Mediterranean. (For more on them, also see my *Paul for Everyone: Galatians and
Thessalonians,* published by SPCK and Westminster John Knox. This
guide is based on that book and was prepared with the help of Patty Pell,
for which I am grateful.)

Therefore, these letters are among the very earliest documents we
possess from the beginning of the church's existence. They are already
full of life, bubbling with energy, with questions, problems, excitement,
danger, and, above all, a sense of the presence and power of the living
God, who has changed the world through Jesus and is now at work in a
new way by his Spirit. Those same qualities can touch us as well as we
delve more deeply into them.

SUGGESTIONS FOR INDIVIDUAL STUDY

1. As you begin each study, pray that God will speak to you through
   his Word.

2. Read the introduction to the study and respond to the "Open" question that follows it. This is designed to help you get into the theme
   of the study.

3. Read and reread the Bible passage to be studied. Each study is designed to help you consider the meaning of the passage in its context. The commentary and questions in this guide are based on my
   own translation of each passage found in the companion volume to
   this guide in the For Everyone series on the New Testament (published by SPCK and Westminster John Knox).

4. Write your answers to the questions in the spaces provided or in a
   personal journal. Each study includes three types of questions: obser-
   vation questions, which ask about the basic facts in the passage; inter-
   pretation questions, which delve into the meaning of the passage; and
   application questions, which help you discover the implications of
   the text for growing in Christ. Writing out your responses can bring
   clarity and deeper understanding of yourself and of God's Word.

5. Each session features selected comments from the For Everyone series. These notes provide further biblical and cultural background and contextual information. They are designed not to answer the questions for you but to help you along as you study the Bible for yourself. For even more reflections on each passage, you may wish to have on hand a copy of the companion volume from the For Everyone series as you work through this study guide.

6. Use the guidelines in the "Pray" section to focus on God, thanking him for what you have learned and praying about the applications that have come to mind.

SUGGESTIONS FOR GROUP MEMBERS

1. Come to the study prepared. Follow the suggestions for individual study mentioned above. You will find that careful preparation will greatly enrich your time spent in group discussion.

2. Be willing to participate in the discussion. The leader of your group will not be lecturing. Instead, she or he will be asking the questions found in this guide and encouraging the members of the group to discuss what they have learned.

3. Stick to the topic being discussed. These studies focus on a particular passage of Scripture. Only rarely should you refer to other portions of the Bible or outside sources. This allows for everyone to participate on equal ground and for in-depth study.

4. Be sensitive to the other members of the group. Listen attentively when they describe what they have learned. You may be surprised by their insights! Each question assumes a variety of answers. Many questions do not have "right" answers, particularly questions that aim at meaning or application. Instead the questions push us to explore the passage more thoroughly.

   When possible, link what you say to the comments of others. Also, be affirming whenever you can. This will encourage some of the more hesitant members of the group to participate.

5. Be careful not to dominate the discussion. We are sometimes so eager to express our thoughts that we leave too little opportunity for others to respond. By all means participate! But allow others to also.

6. Expect God to teach you through the passage being discussed and through the other members of the group. Pray that you will have an enjoyable and profitable time together, but also that as a result of the study you will find ways that you can take action individually and/ or as a group.

7. It will be helpful for groups to follow a few basic guidelines. These guidelines, which you may wish to adapt to your situation, should be read at the beginning of the first session.

    • Anything said in the group is considered confidential and will not be discussed outside the group unless specific permission is given to do so.

    • We will provide time for each person present to talk if he or she feels comfortable doing so.

    • We will talk about ourselves and our own situations, avoiding conversation about other people.

    • We will listen attentively to each other.

    • We will be very cautious about giving advice.

Additional suggestions for the group leader can be found at the back of the guide.

THE FAITH OF
THE THESSALONIANS

1 Thessalonians 1

When the apostle Paul began his letter to the believers in Thessalonica, he recalled his first impressions of them. Thessalonica—modern Thessaloniki, or Salonica—was, and is, a thriving seaport in northern Greece, roughly two hundred miles north of Athens. Paul had come there after preaching in Philippi, further east, where he had been beaten and thrown in prison before pointing out that he was a Roman citizen.

Though Paul's normal practice was to begin his preaching in the Jewish synagogue or place of prayer, it seems that most of the people who came to believe his message were non-Jews. For them, there was a double barrier to be crossed before they could accept the gospel. It was not only a crazy message about a man who was dead and then came to life again. It was a crazy *Jewish* message. Paul must have known, as he went from place to place, that most people who heard what he was talking about were bound to think him mad.

And yet the Thessalonians had not. Some in Thessalonica, as in most places he went, found that something happened to them when they listened to his message. A strange power gripped them—the power that, Paul would tell them, was the Holy Spirit at work.

OPEN

What are some ways different people respond to remarkable experiences—reading an inspiring book, for example, or witnessing an uncommon event?

STUDY

1. *Read 1 Thessalonians 1:1-10.* The church in Thessalonica is probably not many months old. Already they have faced great difficulties; they have been persecuted, and some have died. By way of rooting them more firmly in the gospel, Paul reminds them of what happened when he arrived and preached there.

   What does Paul remember thankfully about the Thessalonians?

2. In verses 3-4 Paul recalls the signs of life he observed among the Thessalonian church, even in the short time he spent with them. What might an accomplishment of faith, the hard work of love or the patience of hope look like in your life or that of your Christian community?

3. As Paul looks back and gives thanks to God for the Thessalonians, he knows that God was indeed at work in them as the word of the

gospel was preached. Why is Paul convinced that God has chosen these believers?

4. What does it mean for the gospel to come in word, in power, in the Holy Spirit, and in great assurance (v. 5) in Paul's day and ours?

5. How did the gospel come to you?

6. The events surrounding the arrival of Paul and his companions in Thessalonica made a remarkable impression upon not only the people who heard and believed the gospel, but on people of all sorts, all around Greece and the neighboring countries. Nobody had to say, "Have you heard about those peculiar Jews who are going around talking about someone called Jesus?"

    What was the story that people everywhere were telling about the Thessalonians?

7. The gods of Greek and Roman paganism were everywhere. If you were going to plant a tree, you would pray to the relevant god. If you were going on a business trip, a quick visit to the appropriate shrine was in order. If you or your son or daughter was getting married,

serious and costly worship of the relevant deity was expected.

At every turn in the road the gods were there: unpredictable, possibly malevolent, sometimes at war among themselves, so that you could never do too much in the way of placating them, making sure you'd got them on your side.

How would "turning from idols" have been an incredibly difficult thing for the Thessalonians to do?

8. What might be parallels for us today of turning away from the "powers" of this world to the one true God and his one true Son?

9. In verses 9-10, Paul describes the conversion of the Thessalonians. What are the elements of conversion Paul describes here?

10. Think of some extraordinary people of faith you have known. In what ways do they seem to influence others, where the only explanation is the power of the living God?

11. In what specific ways can you as a community of believers live in a way that the story of the gospel becomes known around you?

PRAY

Take a moment in silence to picture what it would be like to have others in your neighborhood, workplace or school telling the story of your faith. Spend a few minutes praying for the fulfillment of that picture. Pray for the increase of your faith, love and hope in the midst of all situations so that others will know the gospel message.

2

PAUL'S MINISTRY TO THE THESSALONIANS

1 Thessalonians 2

The ancient world had its fair share of wandering salesmen, traveling teachers, people who tried to make a living by offering their hearers fresh wisdom or insight, some kind of magic, a new philosophy, or whatever. When Paul and his companions arrived in a city and began to tell their strange story, many people must have thought that's the sort of people they were. The cynical ones in the crowd would be waiting for the moment when the speakers produced a moneybag and requested contributions, or invited people to pay to hear more in private.

In a passage that ought to be written out in large letters and hanging on the wall in every Christian minister's house or, perhaps better, engraved in letters of gold on his or her heart, Paul reminds the Thessalonians that his pattern of life has nothing to do with the tricks people would have expected from him.

OPEN

What preachers or teachers have you known or heard of who seemed to be more interested in money than in the instruction or knowledge they had to offer?

STUDY

1. *Read 1 Thessalonians 2:1-20.* In verses 1-2, Paul describes his previous ministry experiences. How did these episodes affect Paul's ministry to the Thessalonians?

2. Perhaps the most remarkable thing about Paul's missionary work is that when he arrived in a new town the people there had quite literally never seen anything of the sort before. They had seen other traveling teachers, but none like this. None of them had behaved as Paul did.

   What are the unhealthy or ungodly motivations for ministry that Paul mentions in verses 3-7?

3. What motives does Paul say drive him and his companions to minister to the Thessalonians and to preach the gospel even in the midst of opposition?

4. Paul contrasts the godly motivations that can drive one to preach the gospel with the self-serving motivations of those who also may be in ministry. It's easy to point fingers, but we all wrestle with these same unhealthy motivations. How do you see mixed motives at work in you when it comes to Christian service?

5. In his dealings with the Thessalonians, Paul could afford to be gentle, caring and loving. He wasn't secretly out to gain anything from them; he simply and genuinely wanted the love of God to embrace them, and as he worked among them he found that his own love was drawn to them as well.

   In what specific and concrete ways mentioned in verses 9-12 did Paul and his companions minister to or disciple the Thessalonians?

6. The central thing that Paul wants the Thessalonians to do (v. 12) is, literally, to "walk worthy of God." The word *walk* is a regular Pauline word for "behavior," following the standard use of the equivalent Hebrew word. Behavior is seen as a matter of putting one foot in front of another; good behavior is taking care of the direction and placing of those feet.

   How do the example and ministry of Paul, Silvanus and Timothy help to encourage the Thessalonians to behave "in a manner worthy of the God" who calls them?

7. An old poem could sum up Paul's life of example in this way:

I'd rather see a sermon than hear one, any day;
I'd rather one would walk with me than merely show the way.
The eye's a better pupil, more willing than the ear;
Fine counsel is confusing, but example's always clear.

Do you agree or disagree? Explain.

8. If someone had cut off 1 Thessalonians at verse 13 of chapter 2, we would have the sense of clear skies, beautiful views and everything in the young church developing straightforwardly. Alas, things are not usually like that in the kingdom of God on earth today. There is a struggle going on, and those who give their allegiance to Jesus as Messiah and Lord will become involved in it whether they like it or not.

Paul's own struggles have been clear from early on. He had been beaten and imprisoned in Philippi, and there was much opposition when he worked in Thessalonica itself (2:2). But now in verses 14-16 we hear that the Thessalonians, too, have already suffered for their newfound faith. And this suffering is evidence of the work of God in their lives.

Suffering is a reality in our world today for believers. How does the church today react to suffering?

9. It is important to realize that when Paul says "Judaeans" here he doesn't simply mean all Jews. He himself was a Jew, as were all the very first Christians. But Paul knows, because he was part of the

movement himself, that within Judaea many Jews had been bitterly opposed not only to Jesus, resulting in their authorities handing him over to the Romans for crucifixion, but also opposed to the groups that sprang up after his resurrection, hailing him as Messiah and Lord.

Believing passionately that God's salvation was for them only, these Jews regarded as blasphemous the message of a crucified Messiah who offered salvation on equal terms to Gentiles as well. What reasons do people have today for not wanting this message promoted?

10. Paul draws on the biblical idea of God's wrath to address the rejection of Jesus by these Jews. God's anger is never capricious or malevolent; when humans reject him, and behave in ways that undermine his wise and generous designs for them and the world, he does not instantly punish but allows space for repentance. When there is no repentance, at some point God says "enough."

We are often uncomfortable discussing God's wrath. How do different churches or different people in the church today respond to the idea of God's wrath?

11. Paul begins to look forward in verses 17-20. He begins to look to the great coming day, the day when Jesus will be revealed once more and so will be personally present with his people, and as Lord of the world. Paul looks forward to the future and in this future takes confidence in the Thessalonians.

Why does Paul refer to the Thessalonians as his hope, joy and crown?

12. Paul exhorted the Thessalonians like a sports coach telling his team
    how to win; he encouraged them like a friend strengthening some-
    one facing a daunting task; he testified to them like a witness in a
    court of law. He lost no opportunity to explain to them that the liv-
    ing God wanted living human beings to reflect his glory, and that
    he had called them, summoned them, bidden them to this utterly
    demanding, but utterly rewarding, way of life.

    But he didn't just use words. The whole point of the first main sec-
    tion of this chapter is that Paul was telling them all this by his own
    example.

    What aspect of the Christian life can you model well for those
    around you?

13. The second section of the chapter (vv. 13-20) shows that for Paul
    the work of love has meant the founding and nurturing of churches,
    as the substantial sign that the living God has indeed been at work
    through him. Of course, there are thousands of different Christian
    callings, most of them not nearly so spectacular and obvious as
    Paul's.

    Each of us has our own work of love to perform, whether it be quiet
    and private or well known and public. What do you think God has
    asked or might be asking you to do? Why?

PRAY

Take a moment to pray for those people in whom you have invested, whether in a quiet, unnoticed way or in a public way. Pray for their growth and maturity in Christ. Pray that you would have the strength and courage to exhibit for these people the characteristics of Christ which you identified in question 12.

3

PAUL'S PRAYER
FOR THE THESSALONIANS

1 Thessalonians 3

Parents lie awake at night and worry about their children. This is how it has always been, and we may assume that it's part of normal human life. Often children don't realize how much the parents are thinking about them, being concerned for their welfare, turning over in their minds all the things that might happen to them. Thus it was with Paul, in Athens with Silvanus and Timothy, as his thoughts about the Thessalonians overflowed, and he felt obliged to send Timothy to find out how they were getting on.

OPEN

Think of a fellow believer whom you hold dear. When you pray for them, what is the content or substance of your prayers?

STUDY

1. *Read 1 Thessalonians 3:1-13.* One of the main reasons that Paul wrote the letter to the Thessalonians was to respond to Timothy's report about the church there. In verses 1-5, what were the reasons that Paul sent Timothy to the Thessalonians in the first place?

2. According to Paul in verses 1-5, how should believers approach suffering?

3. Paul's basic fear was that the Thessalonians may have been swept off track, like a ship blown away from its proper course, or like someone lured away from their proper path by enticing words.

   How can suffering sweep believers off track or lure them away from the proper path?

4. Paul is afraid of compromise, of the Thessalonians abandoning their firm hold on the gospel, their unswerving faithfulness or loyalty to their newfound faith. In the face of the difficulties of the world today, what might compromise look like for the church?

5. In verses 6-10, Paul expresses great joy and thankfulness because of the Thessalonians. What has Timothy reported about the church that has given Paul this deep joy?

6. The Thessalonian church was a new community of faith and love where people from different social, cultural and racial backgrounds treated each other with the love appropriate within a family! This was a sign, which Paul regularly celebrated, of God's dramatic work, starting something quite new, the like of which the world had not seen.

   What expressions of faith and love within your own life or the life of your Christian community today would prompt the same kind of joy and thankfulness that Paul felt?

7. In verse 10, Paul does not say that there is anything wrong with the Thessalonians' faith at present; he only implies that faith needs to grow with every day, with each new trial or test, and that maybe his own further teaching and encouragement will be needed to help that to happen.

   In what ways can the content, passion and pattern of Paul's prayer be a model for us?

8. What are the elements of Paul's beautiful prayer for the Thessalonians in verses 11-13?

9. In what ways is Paul's prayer a reflection of Paul's desire for the Thessalonians both in the present and in the future?

10. Paul understands how important it is to strengthen one another in the midst of suffering so that all believers can stand firm in their faith. What specific steps can you or your Christian community take to help strengthen someone who is in the midst of suffering or difficulty?

PRAY

Spend a few moments giving thanks for the faith and love that you see in your Christian community. After a few minutes of thanksgiving, move into praying for those in your life who are experiencing difficulty. Pray the three aspects of Paul's prayer found in verses 11-13: that you might be able to be present with them, that their love would increase and that they would be strengthened.

4

Instructions on Holy Living

1 Thessalonians 4

Sometimes people whose parents or teachers have seemed impossible to please when they were growing up think of God as someone who will barely be satisfied with our best efforts. Others are so anxious about not being justified "by works" that they imply that we can never do anything at all that pleases God, even as Christians indwelt by the Spirit. Both of these extremes can cause a false understanding of what it means to "please God."

OPEN

When you think about "pleasing God" what is your reaction or what response is evoked?

STUDY

1. *Read 1 Thessalonians 4:1-18.* Paul urges the Thessalonians to behave in a manner that pleases God. What kind of a life do verses 1-8 say is pleasing to God?

2. God longs for us to become the sort of humans who will truly reflect his image. When he sees this happen, he is delighted, like a wise and generous parent with a child who starts to be a cheerful and responsible member of the family.

   What is the connection in verses 1-8 between pleasing God and being sanctified or holy, which is mentioned three times?

3. The first practical area of a holy life that Paul discusses is sexual sin. In verses 3-8 what are the instructions that Paul gives to the Thessalonians regarding this area of life?

4. What kinds of instructions and cautions might Paul give to the church today in the realm of sexuality?

5. Verses 9-12 are often misunderstood as statements about having a kind and winsome spirit in personal relationships, which is to be greatly prized but is not the focus of these verses. In fact I think it is best to translate the beginning and end of these verses as, "Now, about charitable concern for the whole family . . . so that none of you may be in financial difficulties."

   In light of this, how does Paul say love or charitable concern is to be expressed within the church and outside of it?

6. The first Christians, in Jerusalem, sold their property, pooled their resources and shared the money thus gained among themselves (see Acts 2:44-45). This was not simply, as is sometimes said, because they expected the return of Jesus and the end of the world very soon. Many monastic communities, including the one that produced the Dead Sea Scrolls, have had similar practices without such a reason. It was more because the early Christians saw themselves as members of a *family,* and families in the ancient world shared all things in common, often a business as well as a home, helping each other financially as need arose. As the gospel spread around the Mediterranean world, there was no requirement to sell property. But if the gospel meant what it said then Paul said Christians should still regard themselves as a single family.

   How does Paul hold together love, which is expressed through financial giving, and responsibility within the family of the Thessalonians in verses 9-12?

7. Outsiders, looking at a movement that made striking claims about Jesus as Lord of the world, would be interested to see what effect it had on the behavior of the members. They would have seen the Thessalonians living a life of practical love, taking care of one another financially and extending their outreach to the other churches of Macedonia.

Think about your Christian community. What are outsiders seeing as they witness the lives of your community?

8. In what concrete and practical ways can you show your love through financial giving personally and corporately?

9. Along with sex and money, the third practical issue that Paul discusses with the young Thessalonian church in this chapter is death. What are the issues that the Thessalonians are concerned about in verses 13-18?

10. Now put yourself in Paul's shoes as he tries to tell the Thessalonians what is going to happen at the return of the Lord. Paul is concerned that they learn appropriate Christian grief, instead of the wild and hopeless mourning that typified pagan funerals. Paul therefore needs to describe the moment when God makes his new world.

How is the grief of Christians still truly grief but grief with hope instead of hopelessness?

11. Paul's purpose in verses 13-18 is not speculation about the future but comfort in the present so that believers can be confident in God's future purposes for all who have died. There will be grief, but there is also hope. There will come a day when God will put all wrongs to rights, when all grief will turn to joy. Jesus will be central to that day, which will end with the unveiling of God's new world. There, those who have already died, and those who are still alive, will both alike be given renewed bodies to serve God joyfully in his new creation.

Verse 14 repeats one of the earliest Christian creeds, "Jesus died and rose." Because we know he has defeated death and now has a new, resurrected body, we can have the same hope. How should this knowledge of the future make a difference in the way we live now?

PRAY

Pray for your Christian community to have the strength and courage to live holy lives through pure sexual practices, charitable giving and a hope in the resurrection.

NOTE ON 1 THESSALONIANS 4:13-18

Paul joins together several pictures from the Old Testament, and says (vv. 16-17) that the Lord will come down from heaven, accompanied by various dramatic signs. The dead will rise; those who are left alive will be caught up to meet the Lord in the air. These two verses have had a huge influence in some circles where "the rapture" is assumed to be the main Christian hope, with people being suddenly snatched out of homes, jobs, cars and airplanes, leaving the rest of humankind suddenly bereft.

To read the passage like that is a mistake. The key is to realize what *resurrection* itself means: it doesn't mean disembodied life in some mid-air "heaven," but the reembodiment of God's people to live with and for God in the new, redeemed world that God will make. It would therefore be nonsense to imagine that the presently alive Christians are literally going to be snatched up into the sky, there to remain forever. How would they then be with the others who, having died previously, will be raised and given new bodies?

When Paul talks of Jesus "descending," he doesn't suppose that Jesus is physically above us at the moment. Heaven, where Jesus is, isn't another location within our space, but another *dimension*. The language of "descending" is a risky metaphor—all metaphors are risky when talking of the future—that Paul here chooses. Elsewhere (e.g., Colossians 3:4) he can speak simply of Jesus "appearing," emerging from the presently hidden world of heaven, as heaven and earth are at last united, visibly present to one another. Here he builds into the picture, confusingly for later readers, an echo of Moses going up the mountain, the trumpet blast as he is given the law, and coming down again (Exodus 19:16-25).

So when Paul talks of Christians "being snatched up among the clouds," he is again not thinking of a literal vertical ascent. The language here is taken from Daniel 7, where "one like a son of man" goes up on the clouds as he is vindicated by God after his suffering—a wonderful image not least for people like the Thessalonians who were suffering persecution and awaiting God's vindication. And their "meeting" with the Lord doesn't mean they will then be staying in midair with him. The image and language Paul uses would remind his readers of the way Roman citizens in a colony would go out of the city to meet the emperor

as he approaches the town to pay them a state visit. Then the citizens
would accompany the emperor back to the city itself. Likewise we will
meet Jesus and then accompany him back to the new earth over which
he will reign.

CHILDREN OF LIGHT

1 Thessalonians 5

As children, we learn a language from listening to and speaking to those around us. It is only later that we find out there is a grammar behind the language. Likewise, we start acquiring a new skill or learning a new sport just by watching and doing. Only later will we find out that there is a sort of physical grammar—a set of rules or principles to guide how the game is played. When we learn these we find we can play much better than before.

When we are young we learn many other ways to behave in our family and neighborhood and society from being around others as well. At the beginning, we assume these examples, whether they be good or bad, are how we should act as well. Later we find there may be another "grammar" we should learn instead.

OPEN

Consider the process of learning a new language or sport or imitating behavior. How are these processes a good example of the Christian life?

STUDY

1. *Read 1 Thessalonians 5:1-28.* In verses 1-11, what are all the pictures or images that Paul uses to try to explain the relationship between believers and the world and the coming day of the Lord?

2. How does Paul contrast the people of the day and the people of the night?

3. Paul's point about staying awake belongs not so much with the danger of burglars but with the all-important difference between the old world (of darkness, sin and death) and the new world (of light, life and hope).

   What aspects of living as children of the light or children of the day are challenging?

4. The Thessalonians were already children of the day, children of light. God's new world had broken in upon the sad, sleepy, drunken and deadly old world. In verse 11 Paul encourages the Thessalonians to continue to "strengthen one another, and build each other up."

   In what practical ways can the community of believers you are part of encourage each other to live out verses 8-11?

5. As with learning a new language, the grammar is the starting point but the ideal is to reach a point where one does not even need to think about the grammar or the construction of sentences. This is the point of fluency, and it is the same as learning the new language of Christian behavior. The ideal is that believers should have the new language of Christian behavior written on their hearts.

   How are we to relate to Christian leaders as we learn fluency in the new language of behavior for believers (vv. 12-13)?

6. What role does the whole community play in bringing believers to a point of fluency in their behavior (vv. 14-15)?

7. Describe a time when your Christian community affected an aspect of your behavior, causing you to live more as a child of light.

8. Verses 16-22 may well be a list of little rules of grammar, the rhymes and memory aids that are easy to memorize and which nudge the mind in the right direction toward fluency of Christian behavior.

   How would these instructions have specifically helped the Thessalonians in the midst of their grief and suffering to live as children of light?

9. What are some *rules of grammar* that would be especially helpful in the process of becoming fluent in Christian behavior for your community?

10. What might Paul be trying to communicate by using family terminology three times in verses 23-28?

11. In what ways would the reminder of God's faithfulness in verses 23-28 be an encouragement to the Thessalonians?

12. As his letter closes, Paul returns in 1 Thessalonians 5:8 to the theme of faith, hope and love that he began with in 1:3. How do these draw together the other main themes in the letter such as suffering, grief, joy, family and holiness?

13. What are the main things you take with you from this letter?

PRAY

Spend some time praying that you and those in your spiritual family would take what has been learned about Christian behavior into the heart until it becomes second nature, like a mother tongue.

6

The Coming of Jesus

2 Thessalonians 1

It is difficult for believers today to think back to the very first generation of the gospel, and to recapture the sense of strangeness at this new plant, the church, that was blossoming in the Greek world, to grasp the newness and the amazing nature of the work of God in their lives and hearts. But for those believers the mighty acts of God were fresh in their minds, bringing about incredible gratitude. It is equally important for us to ask ourselves what we are thankful for, what gifts we have received from God's generous hands, and what the signs of God's strange work are in our own day, our own place, our own churches.

OPEN

What are some acts of God's grace in your life or in your community that you are grateful for?

STUDY

1. *Read 2 Thessalonians 1:1-12.* When Paul writes this second letter to
   the young church in Thessalonica he emphasizes not only that he is
   thanking God for them, but that it is utterly right and proper to do so.

   What does Paul see in the church at Thessalonica that is filling his
   heart with gratitude to God in verses 1-4?

2. As verses 4-7 suggest, they were also facing difficulties. It was inevi-
   table that the world would find the church a threat and a challenge
   and would oppose them all it could, because the church was indeed
   the beginning of God's kingdom, which would displace all human
   kingdoms.

   What does it look like to have patience and loyalty in the face of
   these kinds of troubles and suffering?

3. How will God's justice be worked out in the world as seen in verses
   5-10?

4. This passage is about God's justice, not his vengeance. Some trans-
   lations of verse 8 use the word *vengeance,* but today this suggests
   quite the wrong idea. Our world has become bad at distinguishing
   between justice and vengeance. We have rightly been so appalled at

actions driven by the lust for vengeance that we have found it difficult to imagine any punishment not being motivated at least in part
by revenge.

How is justice different from vengeance?

5. For all of us there is a desire to see justice done—a deep sense that
    the world needs to be brought back into balance, not just hurting
    someone because that person hurt you. Think about your own life,
    your community or the world. How do you currently most desire to
    see God's justice done?

6. In verses 5-10, Paul describes for the Thessalonians what future jus-
    tice and the coming of Jesus will look like. How would these words
    have deeply encouraged the young believers?

7. In Scripture, there are many moments of judgment, which are at the
    same time moments of deliverance for those who have clung to the
    God of justice and mercy, and have refused to be sucked into the
    prevailing culture of lies and wickedness.

    What are ways the culture today tells lies about what is evil?

How can we cling in strength and courage to the God of justice in the face of this?

8. What is the substance of Paul's prayer for the Thessalonians in verses 11-12, knowing that they are facing persecution and suffering?

9. Christians cannot be complacent about the final judgment. God's longing is that his grace that has called them by the gospel will now do its full work in them. We are not to appear as people who began to believe but never got around to working out what it might mean in practice.

What does it mean for God to "complete every plan he has to do you good, and every work of faith in power" (v. 11)?

10. This passage brings together Paul's gratitude for the Thessalonians' faith, love and perseverance in suffering with the hope of future justice being worked out on the earth through Jesus. Paul ends with the prayer that God may make them worthy of his call and may complete works of grace in the believers' lives.

Which part of this passage strikes you powerfully right now and why?

PRAY

Spend a few moments praying through your response to question 10. Pray prayers of thanksgiving and praise, of the longing for justice, or for the faith to believe in the complete working of grace in your life or in your community.

NOTE ON 2 THESSALONIANS 1:5-7

The sovereignty of God in grace, producing faith, love and patience in new believers, is matched by the sovereignty of God in judgment. Indeed, without that, grace would be ineffectual and arbitrary. God's righteous judgment (v. 5) will at the end come to the rescue of those who have been loyal to God and the gospel, and have therefore been persecuted by the world that demands allegiance to its own power and its own gods. God, in his justice, will repay those who, out of allegiance to idols and their dehumanizing ways of life, have used violence against his people.

The sufferings the Thessalonians are enduring (see 1 Thessalonians 2:14—3:5), and the patience with which they are bearing them, serve, says Paul, as a sign of this judgment of God. The world, then as now, had many "religions," many cults, many "gods" and "lords" (see 1 Corinthians 8:1-6). If Paul had simply been adding another one to this list, nobody would have minded very much.

But he was clearly not doing that: he was inviting his hearers to turn from all other loyalties and give full allegiance to Jesus, and to the God who has been made known in and through him. When they did, provoking a strong reaction, this was indeed a sign that the message was effective. Grace from the one true God had been at work; those who believed became a sign of it; and gratitude was the appropriate reaction, however paradoxical that might seem in the face of suffering and persecution.

7

THE LAWLESS ONE

2 Thessalonians 2

Stand firm and hold on tight." When did you last hear those words? On an airport bus, on a boat ferrying passengers across a busy river. On a narrow mountain ledge when a sudden storm sweeps by. At a time of movement and danger, a time when something is about to happen which might cause injury or even death. Plant both feet as solidly as you can, take hold of the safety rope or anything else you may be able to hang on to, and brace yourself for the shock.

That is precisely the position Paul is recommending to the young church in Thessalonica. There are troubled times on the way, and like a small boat crossing a turbulent waterway, the little ship of the church is going to be tossed to and fro.

OPEN

Suppose your Christian community is facing troubled times. What would it mean for you to "stand firm and hold on tight"?

STUDY

1. *Read 2 Thessalonians 2:1-17.* What do verses 1-2 suggest might be the reason that Paul writes this second letter to the Thessalonians?

2. Obviously, if by "the day of the Lord" (v. 2) Paul meant "the end of the world," the Thessalonians wouldn't have had to be informed by letter that such an event had already occurred. The Old Testament prophets used "the day of the Lord" to refer to catastrophes that befell Jerusalem within continuing history. So what might Paul be referring to by using this Old Testament phrase?

3. Verses 3-12 have puzzled generations of readers. Paul is viewing events through a sort of telescope with several lenses, which together create an image of the object, magnifying it so that it looks closer than it really is. The style of writing which Paul uses here is like that. He is looking, as we now realize, into the far distant future; the final judgment has not yet taken place, but he sees it through the lens of events which were unfolding in his own times.

   In Paul's day, the Roman emperor Gaius Caligula, who was convinced of his own divinity and angry at the Jews, attempted to erect a statue of himself in the temple of Jerusalem, setting himself against God and making himself a god, nearly triggering a major war with the Jews. Even though this disaster was averted when Caligula was murdered in A.D. 41, apparently Paul, using his telescopic style of writing, sees something similar happening in the future.

What events described in verses 3-8 does he see ahead?

4. In this context, what are the characteristics of the "man of lawlessness" he describes?

5. What parallels or examples do you see in our own society of people or institutions living out the characteristics of the "man of lawlessness"?

6. Paul connects the "man of lawlessness" with the presence of the satan. Describe how the satan works in the world in verses 9-12.

7. What is the relationship between God's activity and mankind's choice that is alluded to in verses 9-12?

8. Many of us have met or are aware of people who create a web of lies around themselves, and come to believe in the false world they have invented. Christians, also, are called to search our consciences daily for lies which we, too, can easily create and come to believe.

What lies in the world or in your own heart today are you tempted to create and believe?

9. In verses 13-14, Paul thanks God for his activity in the Thessalonian believers. What progression of the spiritual life and journey do you see in these verses?

10. From Paul's other writings we know that "the traditions" included the basic facts of the gospel; the central actions of the worshiping church, such as baptism and the Eucharist; and the fundamental principles of Christian behavior, particularly the mutual support he calls *agape*, "love."

How would holding "tight to the traditions" enable the Thessalonians to stand firm in the face of troubled times?

11. What can you and your fellowship do to hold tight to the traditions taught by the apostles in order to face the web of lies that threaten and the troubles that challenge us in the world?

12. In the midst of all the problems with deceiving words the Thessalonians had heard, or prospects of being troubled by the lawless one

and the satan, in verses 13-17 what does Paul want them to focus on about God?

13. We easily suppose that if God is in control, we can relax; or that, if we have to struggle and work hard, it means that God isn't as powerful as we had thought. How do you see God's power being exercised precisely by your standing firm and holding tight?

PRAY

Pray specifically about the actions that you take individually and corporately to hold tight to the traditions of the faith. Pray that God will give you the ability to choose to do these things and the perseverance to maintain them.

NOTE ON 2 THESSALONIANS 2:7

What or who, then, is "the restrainer" or the "one who holds it back" (NIV)? We can't be sure. Paul may be thinking of some Jewish leader who would exercise the kind of restraining influence on the emperor that Herod Agrippa (10 B.C.—A.D. 44) had tried to exercise on his friend Gaius. Or he may be thinking of his own work, called by God to establish churches around the Mediterranean world, and trusting that God would delay the catastrophe long enough for him to complete what he had begun. Or he may have some other restraining influence, or person, in mind, that was clear to him and his readers but remains unclear to us.

8

EXHORTATION
AND STEADFASTNESS

2 Thessalonians 3

Among all the strange dreams that one can have, one of the most frustrating is the dream where one is trying to run but discovers that it is impossible to do so. The attempt to run becomes agonizing, but if the dream ends or changes and the runner is freed, the sense of release is great. Paul must have felt, at times, that when he preached, the word of the Lord was like the runner in a dream: trying to do its work but being held back by strange invisible forces, hardly able to put one foot in front of the other.

OPEN

Where are you experiencing frustration in ministry right now? Where are you feeling like the runner in a bad dream?

STUDY

1. *Read 2 Thessalonians 3:1-18.* It must have seemed strange to the Thessalonians, as brand new Christians, that Paul, the great apostle, through whom God was doing so many remarkable things, should need their prayers. For what reasons does Paul ask for prayer in verses 1-3?

2. Why might Paul need prayer to be rescued from evil and wicked people?

3. Think about Christian leaders you know and the opposition that may result when they shine God's light, even with God's love, in dark places. How can you pray for them as the Thessalonians did for Paul?

4. Looking at verses 4-13, what seem to be some of the challenges or problems that the Thessalonian church is facing as it attempts to live as a "family"?

5. The church was attempting to live as a family through mutual financial support. Paul did not require, as the early church had done, that

converts turn over their property to a common purse. But he did require that all members of a church be committed to sharing with one another as each had need, as would be the case in a Mediterranean family of the period.

How did Paul model among the Thessalonians the kind of communal life that he expected them to follow?

6. How would the exhortations that Paul gives in verses 12-13 have helped the Thessalonians to live a godly life together when there were obviously some among them who were not living as would be expected in a spiritual family?

7. Describe the kind of discipline that Paul encourages in verses 10 and 14-16.

8. In verse 10 Paul recommends that those who won't work shouldn't eat. There are always some who, through age or illness, simply can't work. They must be supported. But those who simply don't want to work should be treated with tough love. In verses 14-16 Paul envisions that, in the tight-knit world of small-town family life known to most of his church members, there were appropriate styles of discipline within a family, ways of making it known to a child or a sibling that a particular kind of behavior was unacceptable.

For our modern world, the idea of church discipline is something with which many Christians may be unfamiliar. Much contemporary culture has reacted so strongly against the abuse of power that the mere suggestion of it conjures up images of people being burned at the stake. We have now so embraced the idea of everyone being free to follow their own way that we recoil from the sort of thing Paul seems to recommend.

What sorts of things are likely to happen in a fellowship that does not include a measured, loving exercise of authority?

9. Paul ends with a claim that this letter was written by his own hand and the Thessalonians can be assured of its authenticity and Paul's authority, especially as they may have received letters that purported to come from him but didn't (see 2:2). He also ends the letter with yet another reference to the Lord's grace.

   In the context in which the Thessalonians were living, why is the grace of the Lord Jesus so important?

10. Where do you and your Christian community feel the need for the grace of the Lord Jesus now?

PRAY

There may be people among your church family who are struggling to live according to the framework of Christian faith. Pray for the grace of the Lord Jesus in their lives.

GUIDELINES FOR LEADERS

My grace is sufficient for you.
(2 Corinthians 12:9)

If leading a small group is something new for you, don't worry. These sessions are designed to flow naturally and be led easily. You may even find that the studies seem to lead themselves!

This study guide is flexible. You can use it with a variety of groups—students, professionals, coworkers, friends, neighborhood or church groups. Each study takes forty-five to sixty minutes in a group setting.

You don't need to be an expert on the Bible or a trained teacher to lead a small group. These guides are designed to facilitate a group's discussion, not a leader's presentation. Guiding group members to discover together what the Bible has to say and to listen together for God's guidance will help them remember much more than a lecture would.

There are some important facts to know about group dynamics and encouraging discussion. The suggestions listed below should equip you to effectively and enjoyably fulfill your role as leader.

PREPARING FOR THE STUDY

1. Ask God to help you understand and apply the passage in your own life. Unless this happens, you will not be prepared to lead others. Pray too for the various members of the group. Ask God to open

your hearts to the message of his Word and motivate you to action.

2. Read the introduction to the entire guide to get an overview of the topics that will be explored.

3. As you begin each study, read and reread the assigned Bible passage to familiarize yourself with it. This study guide is based on the For Everyone series on the New Testament (published by SPCK and Westminster John Knox). It will help you and the group if you have on hand a copy of the companion volume from the For Everyone series both for the translation of the passage found there and for further insight into the passage.

4. Carefully work through each question in the study. Spend time in meditation and reflection as you consider how to respond.

5. Write your thoughts and responses in the space provided in the study guide. This will help you to express your understanding of the passage clearly.

6. It may help to have a Bible dictionary handy. Use it to look up any unfamiliar words, names or places. The glossary at the end of each New Testament for Everyone commentary may likewise be helpful for keeping discussion moving.

7. Reflect seriously on how you need to apply the Scripture to your life. Remember that the group members will follow your lead in responding to the studies. They will not go any deeper than you do.

LEADING THE STUDY

1. At the beginning of your first time together, explain that these studies are meant to be discussions, not lectures. Encourage the members of the group to participate. However, do not put pressure on those who may be hesitant to speak—especially during the first few sessions.

2. Be sure that everyone in your group has a study guide. Encourage the group to prepare beforehand for each discussion by reading the introduction to the guide and by working through the questions in each study.

3. Begin each study on time. Open with prayer, asking God to help the group to understand and apply the passage.

4. Have a group member read aloud the introduction at the beginning of the discussion.

5. Discuss the "Open" question before the Bible passage is read. The "Open" question introduces the theme of the study and helps group members to begin to open up, and can reveal where our thoughts and feelings need to be transformed by Scripture. Reading the passage first will tend to color the honest reactions people would otherwise give—because they are, of course, supposed to think the way the Bible does. Encourage as many members as possible to respond to the "Open" question, and be ready to get the discussion going with your own response.

6. Have a group member read aloud the passage to be studied as indicated in the guide.

7. The study questions are designed to be read aloud just as they are written. You may, however, prefer to express them in your own words.

   There may be times when it is appropriate to deviate from the study guide. For example, a question may have already been answered. If so, move on to the next question. Or someone may raise an important question not covered in the guide. Take time to discuss it, but try to keep the group from going off on tangents.

8. Avoid answering your own questions. An eager group quickly becomes passive and silent if members think the leader will do most of the talking. If necessary repeat or rephrase the question until it is clearly understood, or refer to the commentary woven into the guide to clarify the context or meaning.

9. Don't be afraid of silence in response to the discussion questions. People may need time to think about the question before formulating their answers.

10. Don't be content with just one answer. Ask, "What do the rest of you think?" or "Anything else?" until several people have given answers to the question.

11. Try to be affirming whenever possible. Affirm participation. Never reject an answer; if it is clearly off-base, ask, "Which verse led you to that conclusion?" or again, "What do the rest of you think?"

12. Don't expect every answer to be addressed to you, even though this will probably happen at first. As group members become more at ease, they will begin to truly interact with each other. This is one sign of healthy discussion.

13. Don't be afraid of controversy. It can be very stimulating. If you don't resolve an issue completely, don't be frustrated. Explain that the group will move on and God may enlighten all of you in later sessions.

14. Periodically summarize what the group has said about the passage. This helps to draw together the various ideas mentioned and gives continuity to the study. But don't preach.

15. Conclude your time together with the prayer suggestion at the end of the study, adapting it to your group's particular needs as appropriate. Ask for God's help in following through on the applications you've identified.

16. End on time.

Many more suggestions and helps for studying a passage or guiding discussion can be found in *How to Lead a LifeGuide Bible Study* and *The Big Book on Small Groups* (both from InterVarsity Press/USA).

Other InterVarsity Press Resources from N. T. Wright

The Challenge of Jesus
N. T. Wright offers clarity and a full accounting of the facts of the life and teachings of Jesus, revealing how the Son of God was also solidly planted in first-century Palestine. *978-0-8308-2200-3, 202 pages, hardcover*

Resurrection
This 50-minute DVD confronts the most startling claim of Christianity—that Jesus rose from the dead. Shot on location in Israel, Greece and England, N. T. Wright presents the political, historical and theological issues of Jesus' day and today regarding this claim. Wright brings clarity and insight to one of the most profound mysteries in human history. Study guide included.
978-0-8308-3435-8, DVD

Evil and the Justice of God
N. T. Wright explores all aspects of evil and how it presents itself in society today. Fully grounded in the story of the Old and New Testaments, this presentation is provocative and hopeful; a fascinating analysis of and response to the fundamental question of evil and justice that faces believers.
978-0-8308-3398-6, 176 pages, hardcover

Evil
Filmed in Israel, South Africa and England, this 50-minute DVD confronts some of the major "evil" issues of our time—from tsunamis to AIDS—and puts them under the biblical spotlight. N. T. Wright says there is a solution to the problem of evil, if only we have the honesty and courage to name it and understand it for what it is. Study guide included. *978-0-8308-3434-1, DVD*

Justification: God's Plan and Paul's Vision
In this comprehensive account and defense of the crucial doctrine of justification, Wright also responds to critics who have challenged what has come to be called the new perspective. Ultimately, he provides a chance for those in the middle of and on both sides of the debate to interact directly with his views and form their own conclusions. *978-0-8308-3863-9, 279 pages, hardcover*

Colossians and Philemon
In Colossians, Paul presents Christ as "the firstborn over all creation," and appeals to his readers to seek a maturity found only Christ. In Philemon, Paul appeals to a fellow believer to receive a runaway slave in love and forgiveness. In this volume N. T. Wright offers comment on both of these important books.
978-0-8308-4242-1, 199 pages, paperback